A Winning Attitude

50 Tips to Jump Start Your Attitude

D0558684

Jane Savoie

Published by Jane Savoie International

Printed in the United States of America

Savoie, Jane, 1949-
    A winning attitude : 50 tips to give your attitude a
jump start / Jane Savoie.
    p. cm.
    ISBN-13: 978-1-4243-2884-0
    ISBN-10: 1-4243-2884-5

    1. Attitude (Psychology) 2. Optimism.   I. Title.

BF327.S28 2007   158.1
                           QBI07-600004

Disclaimer of Liability
The purpose of this book is to educate and entertain. The author or publisher does not guarantee that anyone following the suggestions, techniques, tips, strategies, or ideas will become successful. The author and publisher shall have neither liability or responsibility to any person or entity with respect to any loss or damage caused, or alleged to be caused, directly or indirectly by the information contained in this book. While this book is as accurate as the author can make it, there may be errors, omissions, and inaccuracies.

Cover Photo by Rhett Savoie

About Jane Savoie

Jane Savoie is one of the most recognized names in the equestrian world, and for a good reason. Her accomplishments and the breadth of her influence are impressive. She has been a member of the United States Equestrian Team and has competed for the US in Canada, Holland, Belgium, France and Germany. She was the reserve rider for the Bronze medal winning Olympic dressage team in Barcelona, Spain in 1992. She has been long-listed by the USET with several horses and has won nine Horse of the Year awards and three National Freestyle Championships.

Jane is as well-known as a coach, writer, and speaker as she is for her competitive accomplishments. She coached at the Olympics in Atlanta in 1996, Sydney in 2000, and Athens in 2004.

Jane has written five books that have been published both in the US and abroad. They include *That Winning Feeling!*, *It's Not Just About The Ribbons*, *Cross-Train Your Horse*, *More Cross-Training*, and *A Winning Attitude*. Several of these best-selling books have been translated into German, French, Italian, Spanish, Dutch, and Polish. She has collaborated on eight books apart from her own titles. Jane has also produced three instructional DVD series entitled *The Half-Halt Demystified!*, *Riding In Your Mind's Eye*, and *Train With Jane*.

She is a frequent contributor to many national magazines and has been lecturing to and inspiring groups of all sizes since 1992.

For more resources and to subscribe to Jane's free newsletter,
***That Winning Feeling!*, visit www.janesavoie.com**

Author's Note

I've learned over the years just how important it is to have the right attitude. A winning attitude is more important than wealth, education, circumstances, intelligence, your past, your successes, or your failures.

Your attitude is also the one thing in life that you can completely control. You may not be able to choose the hand you've been dealt, but you have total control over how you're going to react to that hand. Attitude is a choice.

I also recognize that sometimes it's difficult to maintain an attitude that lets you live the life you want and truly deserve. To help you with this challenge, I've created this little book, *A Winning Attitude*.

I've purposely made the book small so it's handy enough to keep in your car, put on your desk, or leave on your bedside table. It's filled with 50 tips to help you through the hard times. Pick any page, and use the information to give your attitude a boost whenever you need it.

Live Your Dreams!

Jane Savoie

1.
"Do every job, no matter how small, with the care and high standards that would make you proud to sign your name to your work."
– Benjamin Elkind

This philosophy was my dad's, and I'm so grateful to have learned this lesson from him. I remember the day he said it. He was helping me muck out my horse's stall with the usual tools – pitchfork and wheelbarrow. I thought we had finished and that the stall looked fine. Then, to my surprise, he put on a pair of gloves and hand-picked every single stray "poop". By the time he was done, the stall was a work of art.

So, set a higher standard. Be proud to claim your results in anything and everything, from placing in an athletic event, mowing the lawn, organizing your sock drawer, washing your car, or doing a school or business project.

"The secret of joy in work is contained in one word – excellence. To know how to do something well is to enjoy it."
– Pearl Buck

2.
"Live like there's no tomorrow.
Love like you've never been hurt.
Dance like there's no one watching."
– *Satchel Paige*

Live like there's no tomorrow. How would you spend each day if you only had a month to live? No one is guaranteed tomorrow...so live each day as if there is no tomorrow. Don't live on what Dr. Denis Waitley calls Someday Isle. You know. Someday, I'll get fit. Someday, I'll visit Australia. Someday, I'll learn a new language. Someday, I'll start my own business. Someday, when the kids are grown, I'll start taking care of myself.

Love like you've never been hurt. Let your walls down. Love your significant other, your friends, and your acquaintances with your whole heart. Risk it.

Dance like there's no one watching. Lose your inhibitions. Dance like you do when you're alone in your living room in your underwear. If you're not sure how to do that, just picture Tom Cruise in the movie *Risky Business*.

3.
Love is a verb.

Love does wonders for your winning attitude. Show it! Give your time, your attention, and your knowledge. Loving can be something as simple as taking the time to find a phone number for someone, really listening with your whole heart, looking a friend in the eye when he or she talks to you, volunteering your time, money, or skill to a cause you believe in, mentoring a child, offering a foster home for a sick animal, or creating an amazing dinner for a special person.

"Love is forgiving... Love is for giving..."
– Diane Jung

"Happiness comes more from loving than being loved; and often when our affection seems wounded it is only our vanity bleeding. To love, and to be hurt often, and to love again – this is the brave and happy life."
– J. E. Buchrose

7

4.

"Fall down seven times. Get up eight."

– *Chinese proverb*

Never, never, never quit. It doesn't matter how many times you get knocked down. You only lose when you don't get back up.

One of my friends, Ruth Hogan-Poulsen, totally embodies this concept. She's like one of those kid-size, inflatable clown dolls. No matter how much you knock them down, they bounce right back up. Ruth must have been the prototype for those dolls. I've often told her that her initials (RHP) must actually stand for "Resilient" Hogan-Poulsen.

"I bend, but I do not break."

– *Jean de La Fontaine*

"It's not the size of the dog in the fight. It's the size of the fight in the dog."

– *Magic Johnson*

"It ain't about how hard you get hit. It's about how much you can take and keep moving forward."

– *from the movie Rocky Balboa*

5.
Live your best life by living like a dog.

Think of how you could enrich your life and the lives of the people around you if you simply lived like a dog. What character traits do we associate with dogs? To me, they embody loyalty, joy, enthusiasm, and, above all, unconditional love.

Ahhh. Unconditional love. No matter how impatient, lazy, crabby, petty, or self-centered I might be at times, my dog still adores me. She always thinks I am the finest, most wonderful human being on the face of the earth. To her, I am always the best. I certainly don't want to let her down, so every day I plan to do my utmost to be the person she believes I am. Not a bad goal, wouldn't you say?

6.
Courage is not the absence of fear. Courage is being afraid and doing your job in spite of your fear.

We often beat ourselves up for being cowardly and wish, instead, that we could be fearless. We yearn to be like the person who isn't afraid to switch careers, get out of an abusive relationship, take up a new sport, write a book, or _____. (You fill in the blank.)

The reality is that fear doesn't make you a coward. There's nothing wrong with being afraid. Fear only becomes an issue when it paralyzes you and prevents you from doing something you really want to do.

Wrap your head around the fact that when you move ahead in spite of your fear, you're actually very brave. In fact, courage isn't even the issue for people who aren't afraid. If you're not afraid, there's nothing to overcome.

Besides, if you're not afraid at times, it just means that you're not stepping out of your comfort zone and living big enough.

7.
Dream BIG.

Big dreams have magic to inspire you. Small thoughts and dreams won't motivate you when you run into obstacles and setbacks.

So, jump start your dream machine. Pretend you're a little kid and that you can be and do anything you want. What exciting dreams would be on your list? What would make you get up really early and stay up late because you're so excited and driven by your dreams that you can barely stand it? Does it stir your soul to become a Pulitzer Prize-winning author, an Olympic athlete, a neurosurgeon, a world-renowned artist, a prima ballerina, a star of stage and screen, the next Bill Gates or Mother Teresa?

> **"Reach high, for stars lie hidden in your soul.**
> **Dream deep, for every dream precedes the goal."**
> *– Pamela Vauil Starr*

> **"No dreamer is ever too small; no dream is ever too big."**
> *– Will Rogers*

8.
Forgive.

Holding a grudge destroys your winning attitude. So, give yourself the gift of forgiveness. Forgive the people with whom you are angry. Most of the time, they don't even know you're obsessing over real or imagined hurts. Your anger doesn't affect them at all. It just hurts you by lowering your energy and ruining your attitude.

And while you're at it, you might as well forgive yourself too. You can't change the mistakes you've made in the past. Beating yourself up just prevents you from creating the present and future you deserve.

**"If you haven't forgiven yourself something,
how can you forgive others?"**

Dolores Huerta

**"The hatred you're carrying is a live coal in your heart
– far more damaging to yourself than to them."**

Lawana Blackwell

"'Tis the most tender part of love, each other to forgive."

John Sheffield

9.
Keep those good, good, good, good vibrations.
(to be sung along to the Beach Boys hit)

The Law of Attraction explains why "good vibrations" are important. This law is as universal as the law of gravity. It states that we will attract into our experience that with which we are in vibrational resonance.

Bob Doyle, creator of the *Wealth Beyond Reason* program, explains the Law of Attraction in the following way:

> Energy attracts like energy. So when your thoughts and emotions are about joy, gratitude, wealth, and abundance, you literally draw those things to you like a magnet. (By the same token, if your thoughts and emotions are primarily about poverty, lack, fear, and stress, you draw those things to you.) Make a choice to have good vibrations so you can enjoy all the abundance, happiness, health, and wealth you deserve.

"The greatest prayer you could ever pray would be to laugh everyday. For when you do, it elevates the vibrational frequency within your being such that you could heal your whole body."

Ramtha

13

10.
You alone are responsible for your own emotions and attitudes.

No one can make you feel bad. No one can hurt your feelings. You have to give people permission to upset you. So, the choice to get upset is all in your hands. Refuse to give others the power to have that kind of control over your emotions.

"No one can make you jealous, angry, vengeful, or greedy – unless you let him."
Napoleon Hill

"Happiness is available. Help yourself."
Thich Nhat Hanh

"Three grand essentials to happiness in this life are something to do, something to love, and something to hope for."
Joseph Addison

11.
Annihilate fear
with an attitude of gratitude.

Ninety-nine percent of the things we fear never come to pass. So why waste all that energy worrying about things that will probably never happen. Mark Twain summed it up when he said. "I have been through some terrible things in my life, some of which actually happened."

Instead, destroy fear by adopting an attitude of gratitude. Rather than focusing on what you're afraid of, focus on what you're grateful for. Are you afraid to get on an airplane? Be grateful you have someplace to go. Are you afraid of getting bucked off your horse? Be grateful that you get to spend time outdoors with beautiful animals. Are you afraid of getting sick? Be grateful you're not blind or crippled. Are you afraid of becoming blind or crippled? Be grateful that you have a sharp mind. Are you afraid you're not smart enough? Be grateful you have a loving heart. Maybe you don't like your job? Be grateful you have work so you can pay your bills (...and then go about finding your passion so you can do what you love and love what you do!).

As simply as I can put it, when you start to get overwhelmed by fear, remember these two little words: "Thank you".

12.
"We don't 'get' emotions.
We 'do' emotions."
– Anthony Robbins

Refuse to be a victim! You don't "get" depressed, discouraged, or angry. You "do" depression, discouragement, or anger. You "do" these emotions with a very specific physiology. For example, think of the body language of someone who is depressed. He slouches with shoulders down and chest closed. His eyes are down, and his facial muscles are slack. If he were to speak, his voice would probably be soft and slow. If you mimic the physiology of depression, before you know it, you're going to feel sad.

If you don't like feeling depressed, "do" something else. Action precedes emotion. If you want to be excited instead of depressed, change your body language. "Do" excitement. Throw your shoulders back, smile, fling your arms in the air, dance around ecstatically, sing one of your favorite songs at the top of your lungs, and laugh hysterically at how silly you look. Before you know it, you'll be feeling great!

13.
See problems as opportunities.

The only time you won't have problems is when you're dead. So don't try to avoid them. Be grateful that you have them. See problems as opportunities. After all, if you didn't have them, you wouldn't have to learn new skills, grow as a person, stretch yourself, be creative, and move from your comfort zone to your achievement zone.

**"Difficulties are meant to rouse, not discourage.
The human spirit is to grow strong by conflict."**

– William Ellery Channing

**"He who finds diamonds must grapple in mud and mire,
because diamonds are not found in polished stones.
They are made."**

– Henry B. Wilson

**"All the adversity I've had in my life, all my troubles
and obstacles, have strengthened me...You may not realize
it when it happens, but a kick in the teeth may be the
best thing in the world for you."**

– Walt Disney

17

14.
Your subconscious mind is just waiting for your instructions.

One of the biggest mistakes that we make when we're trying to make changes to our attitude, behavior, or performance is that we direct our energy toward the conscious mind. You know – willpower, iron-jawed determination. The problem with that strategy is that you can only make short-term, temporary changes when you direct your efforts to your conscious mind. To make permanent changes, direct your effort to the part of your brain that truly determines your actions – your subconscious mind.

As Maxwell Maltz says in his ground-breaking book, *Psycho-Cybernetics*, your subconscious mind believes everything you say and imagine, sees it as the goal and tries to make it come true. The subconscious mind works, in part, as a goal-striving mechanism. So, like a guided missile, it'll keep you on the course you've set for it. And you alone are responsible for charting that course by what you see in your mind's eye and by what you claim you want.

15.
Choose happiness.

Abraham Lincoln said, "People are about as happy as they make up their minds to be."

That quote reminds me of a commercial I see on TV for a life insurance company. The commercial features a 93-year-old woman. With a twinkle in her eye, she says, "When I wake up every morning, I have two choices. I can choose to be happy, or I can choose to be sad. I choose to be happy."

Choose happiness. Everything else will fall into place.

**"There is little difference in people,
but that little difference makes a big difference.
The little difference is attitude. The big difference
is whether it is positive or negative."**
– W. Clement Stone

16.

"If the only prayer you ever said was "thank you", it would be enough."

Mesiter Eckhart

Gratitude actually attracts more of the things you appreciate and value into your life.

Write down five things you're grateful for everyday.

Need a bit of help getting started? How about:

The kindness of strangers

Your health

Your dog (cat, horse, bird)

Not having to cook tonight (my personal favorite)

Daydreams

Toilets that flush

Doing a great job and having your efforts appreciated
Music
Your favorite song
A nap
Bright colors
Sunshine
The absence of pain
Electricity
Old friends
White chocolate
Modern appliances
Finding a parking space exactly where you need one
A good book
A hot shower
Savoring the scents of life (flowers, food, the earth, your child's
hair, the barn)
The gift of sight
A gentle breeze
Laughter
Restaurants that deliver
Your plane landing safely
Breathing!

21

17.
Progress not perfection.

Too often we beat ourselves up because we're not perfect. Instead, think of yourself as a W.I.M.P. – a Work In Major Progress. As long as you're moving forward, you're headed in the right direction.

Progress is do-able and measurable. Perfection is unattainable, and, therefore, pursuing it is frustrating and demoralizing. Remember, it's the journey as much as the destination. Enjoy the ride.

> **"I am careful not to confuse excellence with perfection. Excellence, I can reach for; perfection is God's business."**
> – *Michael J. Fox*

18.
Worry is a misuse of the imagination.

It would make sense to worry if by doing so you could change a situation for the better. Unfortunately, all worry does is destroy your attitude. Besides, worrying is so powerful that chances are you'll create whatever scares you.

Roger Lanphear, author of *Wealth Consciousness*, explains that if you worry you won't have enough money to pay your bills, chances are you won't. If you worry that you won't get a certain job, you probably won't. If you worry that you'll get sick, you probably will. It's that simple. If you fixate on something with enough worry, chances are you'll get something pretty darn close to it.

He advises worriers to do the following: "A simple technique can help snap you out of the worry state. The objective is to breathe fast and deep so you take in a lot of oxygen. The general state of worry has a physiological component that is transformed with deep breathing. Do whatever is comfortable to get your breath moving. Run or walk fast. Do push-ups, sit-ups, or other kind of exercise. You'll be amazed what it does for your frame of mind."

"If you can solve your problem, then what is the need of worrying? If you cannot solve it, then what is the use of worrying?"
– Shantideva

19.
Attitude is a choice.

You can't control the hand you've been dealt. But you have total control over how you choose to react to that hand.

When disasters happen, don't ask yourself, "Why me?" Instead, take the lemon you were handed and make lemonade.

Look at the lemon that was handed to Christopher Reeve. Here was an actor and an athlete who lost the ability to do the work and play he loved best. Yet, he made a whole barrel full of lemonade out of his life-altering horseback riding accident. He turned that tragedy around and did triumphant work. He used his celebrity status to make some of the most important contributions of his life – increasing public awareness of the importance of research for spinal cord injuries.

He was a man who truly lived the title of his second book, *Nothing is Impossible.*

"The greatest discovery is that a human being can alter his life by altering his attitudes of mind."
– William James

20.
It's better to do something and fail, than to do nothing and succeed.
– *John Mason*

Dare to risk stepping out of your comfort zone. There's nothing wrong with failing. You need to know what doesn't work in order to discover what does work. Get excited about making mistakes because each failure brings you one step closer to ultimate success.

Besides, you never fail if you learn something along the way. Failing itself is not a disaster. Failing and not learning from your failure is a crime. So, the next time you bomb at an athletic event, blow an exam, lose a sale, get turned down for a project or promotion, ask yourself, "What did I learn from this?"

Here's what you might discover by asking such an empowering question. Maybe you need to learn some relaxation skills so you can perform better under pressure. Maybe you need a tutor or coach to help you prepare for your next exam. Maybe you need to work on your attitude, attire, or presentation before your next sales call. Maybe you need to get more experience in a certain area before you apply for that project or promotion again.

21.
Negative thinking is a contagious disease.

I'm sure you've experienced a scenario like the following. You wake up in the morning and feel pretty good. You're excited about the prospects of the new day. Then you go to work, and everyone is complaining. The weather is awful, the boss is a jerk, the pay is lousy, and some of your coworkers are idiots. Before you know it, you're complaining too, and your attitude is in the gutter.

It's important that you avoid negative people like you'd avoid the plague. Since your attitude determines your altitude in life, surround yourself by positive, happy people. That attitude is contagious as well.

"All that we are is a result of what we have thought. The mind is everything. What we think, we become."
– Buddha

22.

"If you think you can or you can't, you're right."

Henry Ford

One of the most important words to eliminate from your vocabulary is "can't". Nothing will short circuit your ability to get from where you are in life to where you want to be faster than saying, "I can't".

Instead, do what peak performance expert Anthony Robbins says to do. Substitute the word "must" for all your "can'ts". Here's how it works: "I can't get motivated to go to the gym and work out" becomes "I MUST get motivated to go to the gym and work out". "I can't stay on track with my career goals" becomes "I MUST stay on track with my career goals." "I can't find the time to finish this project" becomes "I MUST find the time to finish this project".

While you're at it, Robbins also advises substituting that powerful word "must" for all your "shoulds". Once again, here's how it works: "I should get fit and lose some weight" becomes "I MUST get fit and lose some weight". "I should stay in touch with old friends" becomes "I MUST stay in touch with old friends". "I should spend more quality time with my family" becomes "I MUST spend more quality time with my family". "I should quit smoking" becomes "I MUST quit smoking".

23.
To attract good into your life, act "as if" you already have what you want.

The "as if" principle states that if you want to possess a certain emotion or trait, act "as if" you already do, and it will become yours. So, always project on the outside the way you want to feel on the inside. Act courageous, calm, poised, energetic, kind, or any other quality you desire.

There actually is a very real physiological reason that acting "as if" works. In fact, if you were hooked up to machines that measure biological function like EEG and EKG machines, you'd discover that the readings on those machines when you're acting "as if" you possess a quality are identical to the readings you'd see if you felt that way for real. So, you really can fake it 'til you make it.

24.
Feed your winning attitude on a regular basis.

If you're like me, you eat on a regular basis – at least three or four (or five!) times every day. In fact, if I miss a meal, you can hear me a mile away lamenting either that, "I haven't eaten all day!" or "I haven't eaten since breakfast."

Do you feed your mind with the same regularity? Or do you feed it occasionally and haphazardly?

From the neck down, you're really not worth all that much in dollars and cents. But from the neck up, you have unlimited value. So, schedule feeding your mind with the same regularity that you schedule feeding your body. Start or end each day by reading just one paragraph from a positive, inspiring book. That small habit will make a huge difference in your attitude.

25.
Attitude, not aptitude, determines altitude.
Zig Ziglar

How far you go in life – whether in your sport, your career, your fitness level, or your personal relationships – has very little to do with how smart you are, how talented you are, or how much money you have. Your attitude is the single biggest factor in your success.

In his book, *See You at The Top*, Zig Ziglar tells how a study by Harvard University reveals that 85 percent of the reason that people are successful and earn awards, accomplishments, and promotions in their work is because of their attitude, and only 15 percent has to do with technical expertise.

Yes, it's important to learn the skills associated with your sport or work. But the one who excels on any given day is the one who has his head on straight.

So, devote as much time to learning how to have the right attitude as you do to learning your craft. Do you need a little help giving your attitude a boost? Try the following: Visualize yourself being joyful. Study happy, enthusiastic, successful people. Mimic the physiology of excitement. Never complain. Instead, only let positive words come out of your mouth.

26.
Believe!

The only reason we don't go after our dreams is because we believe that our abilities are limited. The truth is that the "belief ceiling" is only in our imagination.

The following story illustrates that the "belief ceiling" is only in our minds. A friend of mine tells of taking her students to the circus. At the circus, the kids saw huge elephants who placidly stayed in an open grazing area. They were restrained only by simple pegs and chains. She explained that the reason the elephants didn't just pull up the stakes and run was because of how they were trained as youngsters. When they were little, no matter how hard they pulled, they weren't strong enough to free themselves. After repeatedly having no success, eventually they gave up because they BELIEVED THEY DID NOT HAVE THE CAPACITY TO BREAK FREE. They stayed enslaved by their belief in their own lack of power – just as many of us do not reach our potential because of beliefs that we are not strong enough, smart enough, athletic enough, old enough, young enough, talented enough, or wealthy enough to reach our dreams.

Napoleon Hill said, "Whatever you can conceive and believe, you can achieve." Think about it. If you truly believed that you'd succeed at everything you tried, what would stop you from "going for it"?

"One of ego's favorite paths of resistance is to fill you with doubt." – *Ram Dass*

31

27.
Avoid "stinkin' thinkers."
Zig Ziglar

Have you ever heard of the expression GI-GO? It stands for Garbage In-Garbage Out. If you fill your mind with garbage from the media or from your "stinkin' thinkin'" friends, as Zig Ziglar calls them, then all that can come out is more garbage. Every thought you have has an effect on you. In fact, studies show that if you're depressed, you're even more likely to catch a cold.

Think of it this way. Let's say I walked into your home with a big plastic garbage bag filled with stuff like coffee grounds, chicken bones, onion peels, eggshells, and dirty baby diapers. I turned the bag over and dumped all that trash on your living room floor. Would you say to me, "Thank you, Jane, for dumping all that garbage in my house"? I imagine you'd tell me to get a mop and clean it up!

Well, the garbage that "stinkin' thinkers" dump into your mind is much more harmful than the garbage I dumped in your house. You're wrong if you think their complaining and negative talk can't hurt you. Every thought that goes into your mind affects your body chemistry within a split second. You need to protect your winning attitude at all costs.

28.
Breathe your way to a better attitude.

One of the best and simplest stress busters is to breathe deeply. To breathe correctly, inhale for a slow count of five and exhale for a slow count of five. As you inhale, put your hand on your stomach, and feel it expand. You should feel like your tummy is getting "fat" because you're lowering your diaphragm. Be sure to keep your shoulders down as you inhale. Otherwise, you're actually just breathing shallowly in your upper chest. As you exhale, feel like you're sewing your rib cage together or like you're pulling your navel into your spine.

As you inhale, imagine breathing in positive thoughts and images. As you exhale, expel all the negative garbage from your mind and body. Here are some examples to get you started:

Inhale love. Exhale impatience.

Inhale a bunch of plus signs (+ + +). Exhale a string of minus signs (- - -).

Inhale gratitude. Exhale worry.

Inhale abundance thoughts. Exhale scarcity thoughts.

Inhale joy. Exhale sadness.

Inhale peace. Exhale anger.

Inhale relaxation. Exhale tension.

Inhale confidence. Exhale fear.

29.
Seek out sources of inspiration.

There's a lot of negative garbage in the world. So be sure to actively dilute the negativity that bombards you on a daily basis. Turn GI-GO (Garbage In-Garbage Out) into "Great In-Great Out." Preserve a winning attitude by deliberately seeking out sources of inspiration. Watch uplifting movies, read good books, go to seminars, play motivational CDs, listen to inspiring music, and surround yourself by positive, excited people.

My favorite movies include Rocky and Rudy. I'm a sucker for any book or tape by Anthony Robbins, Denis Waitley, or Zig Ziglar. And I love hanging around possibility thinkers who say, "Let's do it!" rather than, "It can't be done."

**"You can't wait for inspiration.
You have to go after it with a club."**
– Jack London

30.
Set specific goals...and make them big!

It's hard to arrive someplace if you don't know where you're going. When you set clear goals, you create the future in advance. Goal-setting works because whatever you consistently focus on, you eventually experience. As you think, so you create.

Goals not only give you something concrete to work toward but also help you measure your progress along the way.

Set big, exciting goals that are just out of reach but not out of sight. Exciting goals will keep you on track when the going gets rough.

Another reason goal-setting works is that once you define your goal and your brain sees you don't have it, you'll become dissatisfied. That discomfort creates internal pressure that will then prompt you to take positive action.

"I always wanted to be somebody. But I see now I should have been more specific."
Lily Tomlin

31.
Keep your attitude on track by asking high-quality questions.

I learned from peak performance expert Anthony Robbins that the best way to give yourself an attitude adjustment is to ask high-quality questions. When you ask low-quality questions, your brain searches for an answer and can only come up with low-quality answers. Here are some low-quality questions: "Why does this always happen to me?" "Why can't I pay all my bills?" "How come I always end up getting sick whenever anyone around me catches a cold?" The only kind of answers your brain can come up with to questions like that are: "Because the world is out to get you." "Because you're not smart enough to get a better job." "Because you have a terrible immune system."

Notice that low-quality questions often start with the words "Why?" or "How come?" As soon as you hear those words come out of your mouth, stop mid-sentence! Then, ask a better question.

Better questions would be: "What do I need to change in order to create the results I want?" "How can I offer more value with my services or products so I can make more money?" "What do I need to do in terms of nutrition and exercise in order to strengthen my immune system?"

So, when your attitude is in the gutter, get yourself out of your funk by ASKING A BETTER QUESTION such as, "What's good about this?", "What can I learn from this?", or "How can I use this?" Your answers will surely empower you.

> ### "Ask questions from your heart and you will be answered from the heart."
> *Omaha Proverb*

> ### "Judge of a man by his questions rather than by his answers."
> *Voltaire*

32.
Words can transform your attitude – for better or for worse.

To maintain a winning attitude, eliminate the words "not" and "try" from your vocabulary.

Remember, your subconscious is just waiting for your instructions. However, there is no picture in the mind for the word "not." So when you say, "I won't be nervous," or "I will not worry," or " I am not a loser," all your subconscious hears is "I will be nervous," "I will worry," or "I am a loser." If you use the word "not" as you program yourself for success, you'll end up getting the opposite of what you want!

While you're at it, eliminate "try" from your vocabulary. The word "try" carries a built-in excuse. When you "try" to do your best, you're basically admitting that you're not committed to achieving your goal. You can always do your best even though your "best" today won't be your same "best" six months from now.

I feel quite strongly about eliminating the word "try" because of its connotation of a lack of commitment. The following story illustrates my point:

Years ago, I was on a flight from West Palm Beach to Cincinnati. We were just taking off when we were suddenly jolted by two frightening alarms. Within moments the entire cabin filled with smoke. I looked behind me and couldn't see much beyond the fourth or fifth row. The flight attendants were running up and down the aisle. To add to the passengers' panic, no one would tell us what was going on. The atmosphere was charged with terror. Finally, the pilot came over the radio. He didn't tell us what was going on (he probably didn't know either), but what he did say didn't help. I became more panic-stricken as he announced, "We're going to turn around and head back to the terminal...and we're going to try to have a normal landing."

TRY, I thought! You're going to TRY to have a normal landing? You just better commit yourself to landing this thing safely. Obviously he did, but ever since then I've strongly advised people that they take that wishy-washy word "try" out of their vocabulary.

33.
Celebrate shades of gray.

Want to know how to have a good day everyday? Stop expecting perfection. Instead, learn to see things in "shades of gray". The key to seeing shades of gray is to recognize when things are "a little bit better". For example, you've gotten strong enough to lift a slightly heavier weight at the gym. You can jog a little bit faster or a little bit further. You're feeling somewhat more coordinated with a particular skill in a new sport. You passed up that extra doughnut. You've stuck to your resolution to read something positive every day. Your favorite jeans are a little looser. You're treating your friends and significant others a little more lovingly each day. By the way, all those "little bit betters" very quickly add up to a whole lot better.

Invent reasons to celebrate, and then have fun with it. Go out for a special dinner. Treat yourself to a new blouse or gadget. Go to the movies. Buy yourself some flowers. Do something fun, and just make it an occasion!

34.
Choose an attitude of gratitude.

This is one of the best ways to raise your vibrational frequency so you can attract what you want into your life.

Do what Oprah does. Start a gratitude journal. Everyday, jot down five things you're grateful for. If you can't think of five things, at least write down, "I'm breathing!"

If you're having a really bad day, and you ask yourself what you're grateful for, you might end up growling, "Nothing!". If that's how you feel, ask a better question. Ask, "What COULD I be grateful for?" I bet you'll come up with all kinds of answers to that question. I'll get you started. How about your family, petting a dog, eating popcorn at the movies, air conditioning, rocking chairs, days off, your eyes, a cleansing rain, the smell of gardenia. Get the picture?

"A thankful heart is not only the greatest virtue but the parent of all the other virtues."

– Cicero

35.
If your attitude is right, the facts don't matter.

A winning attitude is a powerful force. So powerful, in fact, that when your attitude is right, the "facts" don't matter. The "facts" are all the logical reasons why it would be impossible for you to reach your goal.

Here's my story. One of my big goals was to become a member of the United States Equestrian Team and represent my country in international competition. I couldn't imagine anything more exciting than earning the privilege of wearing my country's flag when I cantered into the arena on my horse. Sounds like a reasonable goal, right?

Wrong. I had a huge list of "facts" that should have made it impossible for me to succeed. Here's a partial list of those "facts". I didn't have a horse. (It's hard to make the Equestrian Team without a horse!) I didn't have any money to either buy or support a horse.

I didn't have a lot of experience since I had only competed at the lowest levels.

I was twenty pounds overweight. I was smoking three packs of cigarettes a day (hardly the picture of an elite athlete!).

Although athletic, I was not a naturally gifted rider. I was very mechanical. I was a very nervous competitor. (I couldn't eat on competition day and spent a lot of time in the Port-O-Let!) I wasn't much of a risk-taker. I preferred the safety of my comfort zone.

Yet, in spite of all these "facts", I achieved my goal. When all was said and done, the right attitude was much more important than all the "facts" that were stacked against me.

43

36.
No matter what, believe in "I can"!

In his book *Psycho-Cybernetics*, Maxwell Maltz tells the well-known story of Roger Bannister and the four-minute mile. Throughout the entire history of sports up to the year 1954, athletes were unable to run a mile in under four minutes. This feat was perceived as a physical impossibility. Then along came Roger Bannister, who believed he could break this barrier – and he did. The interesting fact is that once Bannister succeeded, athletes all over the world were able to do the same. Man had not physically changed. The barrier was broken because it was a mental obstacle rather than a physical one. Once runners believed it could be done, they did it time and time again. Their attitude and belief of "I can" made all the difference.

"In the province of the mind, what one believes to be true either is true or becomes true."
– John Lilly

"They can conquer who believe they can."
– Virgil

37.
You're never fully dressed without a smile.

Today, I heard this line in a song from the musical Annie, and I thought about how true that is. Smiling is a universal language. It's a great way to communicate. And even more importantly, a smile will change your physiology to one of happiness. Remember, action precedes emotion. If you want to be happy, SMILE.

As my husband, in his very Rhett-like way, likes to say, "If you're happy, notify your face!" So, slap a big grin on your face, and enjoy your day! (And as a wonderful byproduct, you'll brighten someone else's day too.)

"Always laugh when you can. It is cheap medicine."
– Lord Byron

"You don't stop laughing because you grow old. You grow old because you stop laughing."
Michael Pritchard

45

38.
Capture a winning attitude by growing and contributing.

Anthony Robbins explains that there are six basic human needs. Most of us live our lives based on two or three of those first four needs, which are the need for certainty, the need for variety, the need for love and connection, and the need for significance.

However, if you want to have a fulfilling life, move yourself from living predominantly in the first four basic human needs into the last two needs – the need to grow and the need to contribute. Growth and contribution make the difference between merely existing and leading a truly fulfilling life.

Grow by becoming a student of life – learn, study, observe, listen, and evolve.

Contribute by mentoring a child. Donate to your favorite charity. Volunteer your time or expertise. Pay the highway toll for the car behind you. Spend time with a needy friend. Teach someone a new skill. Make someone's day by offering a sincere compliment. Carry someone's groceries. Make your mantra, "What can I do to help?"

**"We make a living by what we get.
We make a life by what we give."**

– Maya Angelou

**"We feel that what we are doing is just a drop in the ocean.
But the ocean would be less because of that missing drop."**

– Mother Teresa

**"We are not here merely to make a living.
We are here to enrich the world, and we
impoverish ourselves if we forget this errand."**

Woodrow Wilson

39.
Rejoice in the success of others.

The Law of Abundance confirms that there is enough for everybody. You don't have to be envious or resentful of someone's success. Their success in no way prevents you from having everything you desire. So celebrate for them and with them. You'll raise your own vibration, which, in turn, will help you develop a winning attitude so you can create the life you deserve.

"Abundance can be had simply by consciously receiving what has already been given."
– Sufi Saying

"There are two ways of exerting one's strength: one is pushing down, the other is pulling up."
– Booker T. Washington

"Our envy of others devours us most of all."
– Alexander Solzhenitsyn

40.
Preserve your winning attitude by avoiding gossip.

Gossip might seem like harmless fun. Consider the popularity of the tabloids like the National Enquirer. But the truth is, gossip is an energy-draining disease. Don't listen to it or take part in it. It will lower the frequency of the vibrations of your energy.

Besides, gossip is rarely accurate. The reality is that there are three sides to every story: your side, my side, and the truth.

> **"You can bend it and twist it...**
> **You can misuse and abuse it...**
> **But even God cannot change the truth."**
> – *Michael Levy*

> **"Never tell evil of a man, if you do not know it for certainty,**
> **and if you know it for a certainty, then ask yourself,**
> **'Why should I tell it?'"**
> – *Johann K. Lavater*

49

41.
Take care not to get "hung by your tongue."
– Francis P. Martin

Be mindful about the words that come out of your mouth. Remember, your subconscious mind hears everything you say, sees it as the goal, and tries to make it happen. So, if you put yourself down and say things like you're a klutz, you're always broke, or you have a hot temper, that's exactly what you'll get. You'll be clumsy, in debt, and angry.

Your subconscious doesn't know or care if you're lying. So "lie" your way to the life you want. Say out loud that you're coordinated, you pay your bills comfortably, or you're infinitely patient.

"The most important conversation is the one you have with yourself. So be sure to treat yourself with all due respect."
– Dr. Denis Waitley

42.
Winning is an attitude.

Winning doesn't necessarily mean bringing home a trophy, blue ribbon, or medal. Winning is developing your potential and using it for a purpose that makes you happy. It is leaving your all-too-familiar comfort zone and striving to move into the achievement zone. It is putting out the kind of effort that makes you proud to sign your name to your work. Winning is doing your personal best. It's a feeling and attitude you take with you long after that blue ribbon fades or that trophy or medal tarnishes.

"You don't need to win every medal to be successful."
— Jason Fried

"I'd rather be a failure at something I love than a success at something I hate.
— George Burns

43.
Picture what you want in great detail.

The common denominator of all super achievers is that they have developed the ability to clearly see what they want, in great detail, well before they actually achieve it.

Vivid imaginary pictures change the software in your mental computer. To create the reality you want, fill in details, involve your five senses, and add emotion to your "mental movies".

1. Fill in details. Notice what you're wearing, where you are, what the weather is like, or whether you are alone or in a crowd.

2. Involve your five senses. That is, "see" yourself with that gold medal around your neck, or in that two-story, saltbox home overlooking the Atlantic ocean, or enjoying that huge royalty check for your best-selling novel.

   "Feel" the weight of the medal, the texture of the wood on the railing around the porch, or the pen in your hand as you endorse the check.

"Hear" the roar of the crowd as the medal is placed around your neck, the sound of the waves crashing on the rocks, or the scratch of the pen as it moves across the paper.

"Smell" the crisp clean air on the day you are given your medal, the ocean air, or the ink as it dries.

"Taste" the salty sweat from the effort of your athletic performance, the salt from the ocean, or the ink from the tip of the pen you touched to your tongue.

3. Include emotion in your picture. Experience the pride of winning that medal, the serenity of living in that home, or the security and sense of accomplishment of earning that check.

44.

"You can't fix a bad hairdo by combing your reflection in the mirror."
– Mike Dooley

Do certain people annoy you? I hate to break this to you, but their irritating traits are merely a reflection of the traits you don't like in yourself.

Trying to "fix" other people is like looking in the mirror, seeing that you're having a bad hair day, and trying to fix your hair by combing your reflection!

Instead, figure out what you don't like about yourself, and work on that.

"We don't see things as they are. We see them as we are."
– Anais Nin

"Be the change you wish to see in the world."
– Mahatma Ghandi

45.
Happiness is something you decide on ahead of time.

Dr. Wayne Dyer tells a story of a 94-year-old, nearly blind woman who was being moved to a nursing home. She had to move because her husband of 70 years had just died. On the day of her move, she waited patiently in the lobby of her previous apartment for someone to assist her. When she finally arrived at the new home, she used her walker to slowly and painfully maneuver into the elevator. As she reached her floor, the elevator doors opened, and she exclaimed, "I love it!" The attendant said, "But you haven't even seen your room yet." Her response was, "It doesn't matter how the furniture is arranged. It is all about how I arrange my mind."

"The foolish man seeks happiness in the distance, the wise grows it under his feet."

– James Oppenheim

"Remember that happiness is a way of travel – not a destination."

– Roy M. Goodman

55

46.
Our lives are made rich by the moments that leave us breathless.

Which moments leave you breathless? Maybe it's seeing your newborn baby for the first time, watching a gifted dancer, enjoying a magnificent sunrise, your lover's smile, the joy in your dog's eyes when you come home, watching an athlete break an "unbreakable" record, a symphony, rainbows, seeing your best friend succeed, watching kittens play, seeing a toddler take his first steps, the Grand Canyon, fall foliage, your first sky dive, the Rocky Mountains, wildlife, the look on your children's face on Christmas morning, the kindness of a stranger, when your daughter asked you to walk her down the aisle, or feeling passionate about a person, place or idea.

When your attitude takes a nose-dive, savor those memories. Be grateful for them. They make your life rich.

"Maybe it was only a second of your time, but you need to treasure life, every second."
– Takayuki Ikkaku, Arisa Hosaka and Toshihiro Kawabata, Animal Crossing: Wild World

47.
Move from scarcity thinking to abundance thinking.

You can move yourself from scarcity thinking to abundance thinking through the Law of Attraction. The Law of Attraction is based on quantum physics – the study of subatomic particles (energy). You might ask what that has to do with wealth and happiness. The answer is, "Everything."

You are using the Law of Attraction right now to "attract" everything in your life - even the things you DON'T want! The premise behind the Law of Attraction is that everything around us, including ourselves and our thoughts, is composed of energy. It is a basic law of physics that "like energy attracts like energy".

Therefore, we get more of whatever we think about the most!

So, attract abundance (wealth, health, happiness, prosperity) into your life simply by learning how to harness the power of your thoughts. Conversely, if most of your thoughts are of scarcity, envy, illness, or sadness, you will attract more of that into your life.

48.
Change the Software in Your Mental Computer

I love Albert Einstein's definition of insanity. He says, "Insanity is doing the same thing over and over and expecting a different result". If you want to change your attitude, behavior, skills, or anything else in your life, you need to make changes by installing new software in your mental computer.

The bonus of changing your mental software rather than using will power or iron-jawed determination is that it's a lot easier to do and the results are permanent. All you have to do are two simple things: Program your mind through visualization and self-talk.

Here's all you need to know about visualization:

1. Relax. (Take 3 deep breaths.)

2. Fill in details. (What are you wearing? What do your surroundings look like?)

3. Use your five senses. (Feel the texture of the rug under your bare toes. Smell the citrus-scented candle. Hear the rhythmic ticking of the grandfather clock. See the layout of the furniture in the room. Taste the salt from the cracker you just ate.)

4. Use emotion. (Fully experience the emotion you want, such as being brave, confident, relaxed, or peaceful. To help you do this, just remember another time in your life when you actually felt that emotion.)

5. Repeat daily. (It takes about 21 days to develop a habit.)

Here's all you need to know about self-talk. Always speak to yourself in the following way:

1. Use the present tense as if you already possess the quality you want. ("I am confident, disciplined, organized, or calm.")

2. Use a positive phrase. ("I am relaxed" as opposed to "I am not tense." Remember, there is no picture in the mind for the word "not". So when you say "I am not tense, your mind only hears, "I am tense.")

59

49.
If you're afraid, take action!

Change your attitude toward fear. Fear means you're growing. Every time you stretch yourself, aim a little higher, or take a risk, you're going to experience some anxiety. So fear itself is not the issue. The problem exists only when you become immobilized by your fear.

So, rather than interpreting fear as a signal to retreat, start to think of it as a cue to take action. As you move ahead, you'll find that action cures fear. You see, you might think you're safe if you stay in your comfort zone. But refusing to push through your fears actually leaves you with a greater sense of dread because you feel helpless.

So, take a small risk every day. That's not to say that you should take foolish chances. Always make sure you're well prepared for the task at hand. But taking a well-thought out risk will make you feel great. And even if it doesn't work out, at least you've made an effort. You're not sitting back powerless and immobilized by your fears.

"You gain strength, courage, and confidence by every experience in which you really stop to look fear in the face... You must do the thing you think you cannot do."

– Eleanor Roosevelt

50.
STEP UP!

I have a poster hanging in my office that I'd like to share with you.
I hope it moves and inspires you the way it does me. It comes from
Anthony Robbins, author of *"Awaken the Giant Within"*.

Repeat each of the following sentences out loud.
Say it with intense feeling, and allow your voice to get
progressively stronger with each line.

Now I Am The Voice!

I Will Lead, Not Follow.

I Will Believe, Not Doubt.

I Will Create, Not Destroy.

I Am A Force For Good.

I Am A Leader!

Defy The Odds!

Set A New Standard!

STEP UP!

STEP UP!

Give the gift of A Winning Attitude to the people you love.

A Winning Attitude

50 Tips to Jump Start Your Attitude

by Jane Savoie

A winning attitude is more important to your success than any other single factor. You may not be able to choose the hand you've been dealt, but you have total control over how you're going to react to that hand. Yet, there are times when it's difficult to maintain an attitude that lets you live the life you truly want and deserve. To help you with this challenge, Jane has created this little book to help you through the hard times. Pick any page, and use the information to give your attitude a boost whenever you need it.

$11.95

Special Quantity Discounts

5-20 Books .... $9.00 each	100-499 Books .... $7.00 each
21-99 Books .... $8.00 each	500-999 Books .... $6.00 each
	1,000+ Books .... $5.00 each

**To place an order, visit www.janesavoie.com
or email jsavoie@mindspring.com**

Jane Savoie

The Perfect Speaker for Your Meeting or Seminar!

Here's what the experts say about Jane:

"Don't miss an opportunity to be in the same room with Jane Savoie! She is articulate and upbeat, and can make the most complex concept easy to understand and apply. As a hard charging executive, I appreciate the wisdom of a speaker who can get right to the bottom line with solid advice and practical solutions. Jane knows how to deliver, and with a positive punch that will motivate you to take action!"
– Saly Glassman, Merrill Lynch, Senior Vice President-Investments

"You only have to see Jane enter the room to recognize that this lady has comfortable self-confidence and composure. You only have to listen to her opening comments to realize that she is as down to earth as she is enthusiastic...Savoie will charge your batteries."
– Dressage and CT magazine

©Nan Rawlins for Equimage® Media

"Jane Savoie doesn't just know about winning horse shows - she knows about winning. Even when she is talking about her success in the equestrian world, she is speaking to the winner in all of us, even if our only sport is the game of life."
Brad Yates, Speaker and Co-author of the bestseller
"Freedom at Your Fingertips"

Jane Savoie has an amazing ability to zero in on the core of a problem, and give you the solution in a clear, no-frills way.
Sue Blinks, United States Equestrian Team,
Olympic and World Championship Bronze and Silver Medalist

www.JaneSavoie.com

To schedule Jane to bring
That Winning Feeling
to your next event, contact her at
jsavoie@mindspring.com
or visit **www.janesavoie.com**

Add Jane's Other Peak Performance Books to Your Library.

That Winning Feeling! $14.95
Program Your Mind for Peak Performance
Encompassing the areas of dressage, eventing and show jumping, Jane presents a revolutionary approach to riding by which you can train your mind and shape your attitudes to achieve higher levels of skill.
"This is a book that you must read, whether you ride dressage, cow horses, or just trail ride..."
– *Quarter Horse Journal*

It's Not Just About The Ribbons $24.95
It's About Enriching Riding and Life with Innovative Tools and Winning Strategies
"If you have lost the riding confidence you once had as a child or have been developing setbacks with your horsemanship, *It's Not Just About The Ribbons* could hold the answers to how you can move forward and improve. This book holds a lot of informative advice, teaching you how to develop your mind to work for you, not against you. For anyone wishing to develop their mental skills to overcome those emotions that develop barriers when riding, this could be the book for you."
– *The British Horse Society*